A
CLASSICAL
MASTERPIECE

By
Devon L. Sanderson

TEACH Services, Inc.
P U B L I S H I N G
www.TEACHServices.com

Copyright © 2009 Devon L. Sanderson
Copyright © 2009 TEACH Services, Inc.
ISBN-13: 978-1-57258-2550-8
Library of Congress Control Number: 2009931155

Published by

TEACH Services, Inc.
P U B L I S H I N G
www.TEACHServices.com

DEDICATION

A Classical Masterpiece is dedicated to the memory of my dearest and loving mother, Josephine Scarlett-Vaccianna who came into this world on April 11, 1928 and departed this life on March 03, 2007. And to my thoughtful and caring cousin, Adre Shakes-Crawford who came into this world on July 05, 1939 and departed this life on September 27, 2008.

Both my mother and my cousin contributed to my life in no ordinary way—significantly. Their meager resources and loving sacrifices did a lot for me. Their indelible touches will stay with me forever. They both influenced my life in a most remarkable way. Moreso, they directed me to always reflect on King Solomon's words of wisdom: "Trust in the Lord with all thine heart and lean not unto thine own understanding. In all thy ways acknowledge Him and He shall direct thy paths. (Proverbs 3:5, 6). These wise words will keep me on the straight and narrow path, until we meet again. May their souls find eternal peace.

—The author.

(12.05.'08)

GRATITUDE TO GOD

I am grateful to God for having inspired me to write this book. I believe I have been truly inspired. To Him be the glory, honor and praise.

— The author.

(03.05.'08)

TABLE OF CONTENTS

ACKNOWLEDGMENTS

I wish to extend my profound gratitude to those who gave me encouragement and whose invaluable efforts helped make *A Classical Masterpiece* a reality. To Christine Campbell who typed the manuscript so ably. To my wife, Pauline, who asked me no questions when I sat up late at night to proof read the final draft. Finally, thanks to the publishers for a job well done.

—The author

GOD'S CREATION

God is great, wonderful, creative!
Natural beauty and splendor of each new day
The ultra-violet rays of the sun
Testify of the Creator's love.

Human inventions combined with the Divine
Bring joy and satisfaction to
The minds of the broad families
Of the universe in observation of His magnificent grace

Swaying trees, majestic view
Of the landscape and the silent
Flowing streams expressing
Generous, unfeigned appreciation

The atmospheric power–nature
So firmly revealing its Maker.
As humans born from the image
Of the All-powerful, there is need

To praise and worship Him for
It is pleasant with acceptance that
Everything is marvelously
And curiously made.

INSPIRATION

Inspiration is an insight
From deep within or a
Direct contact with the Divine;
Its messages are significant.

Inspiration teaches wisdom,
Goodness and life's expectancies,
It teaches what the eyes
Cannot see nor the mind perceives.

Inspiration is more than
Intellectual knowledge,
It is not related to practical
Nor theoretical pursuits, or timely research.

Inspiration exceeds human
Thinking and findings
It is more valuable than
The highest degree achieved.

Inspiration brings peace
And happiness to the entire
Being which cannot
Be easily compared.

IT IS SPRING!

It is springtime again
And Nature is happy
With the newness of
This beautiful season.

New plants are springing up
Birds and other little creatures
Are 'boasting' the fact
That the season is here.

The freshness of the air,
The blooming of flowers,
And the warmth of the
Sunshine testify of this season.

There is green grass
For the animals to eat,
And the forests are
Enjoying the rain, too.

In the four seasons of
The year, sowing and reaping
Are done but…
Spring is great harvest time!

AN ACRONYM

(Jody-Anne Maxwell, Jamaican,
1998 Scripps Howard Spelling Bee Champion).

J *ustice must be given when the occasion arises.*
O *utlook on positive lifestyle brings satisfaction.*
D *edication combined with loyalty and practice bring excellence.*
Y *ou possess high intelligence by virtue of perseverance.*

A *chievement comes through discipline and determination.*
N *ecessity is the key to open up successes.*
N *ever allow anything to deter your aspirations and goals.*
E *ternal rewards begin in this life.*

M *uch is gained when much is given.*
A *nswer to duties even in challenging times.*
X *is for good examples to follow.*
W *hen good listeners listen they will learn.*
E *xceptional intellect is very rare.*
L *earn to love even the unloveables.*
L *ean on God, He is your Source of knowledge.*

THE WESTERN MIRROR

(The Mirror's Twentieth Anniversary Celebration —2000).

The plan was unsettled,
The minds behind such a
Significant, remarkable idea
Were not made known.

It could be the erection
Of a museum or a monument,
Or a magnificent cathedral,
But it was none of these.

As the idea came into being,
The journalistic efforts stood
Firm for the establishment
Of an indefinite newspaper.

A newspaper that would
Withstand the test of time;
Even one that would endure
Much longer than the Beacon.

What more appropriate name
For a news highlight
For the people of the West
But the Western Mirror!

We the people who crave
For knowledge as an interest,
Look for each publication—
As it leaves the press each time.

It is not a daily publication,
It is not circulated nationally,
It may not seem important,
But it is most informative.

The Western Mirror is
Faithfully keeping the people
In the West abreast for
Twenty consecutive years.

Let us, the people of the
West, then celebrate the existence
Of this noble newspaper.
Long live the MIRROR!

CURAÇAÓ

Nestled away in the Netherlands
Antilles is the small island of Curaçaó.
This small island's capital is Willemstad,
With three of the world's most beautiful
Bridges— Juliana, Emma and Wilhelmina.

The natural resources—the people—
Are rare—a quality hard to find
Elsewhere in the Caribbean.
Beautiful, honest and pleasant
Are only a few of the words to describe
Those people of linguistic ability.

It is a memorable experience
For anyone to be on this
Charming island, whether you
Are vacationing, shopping or
Transacting business in any aspect.

The atmosphere is ever serene
And tranquil, under the starry heaven
Curaçaó is a dream come true
For visitors from the world over.

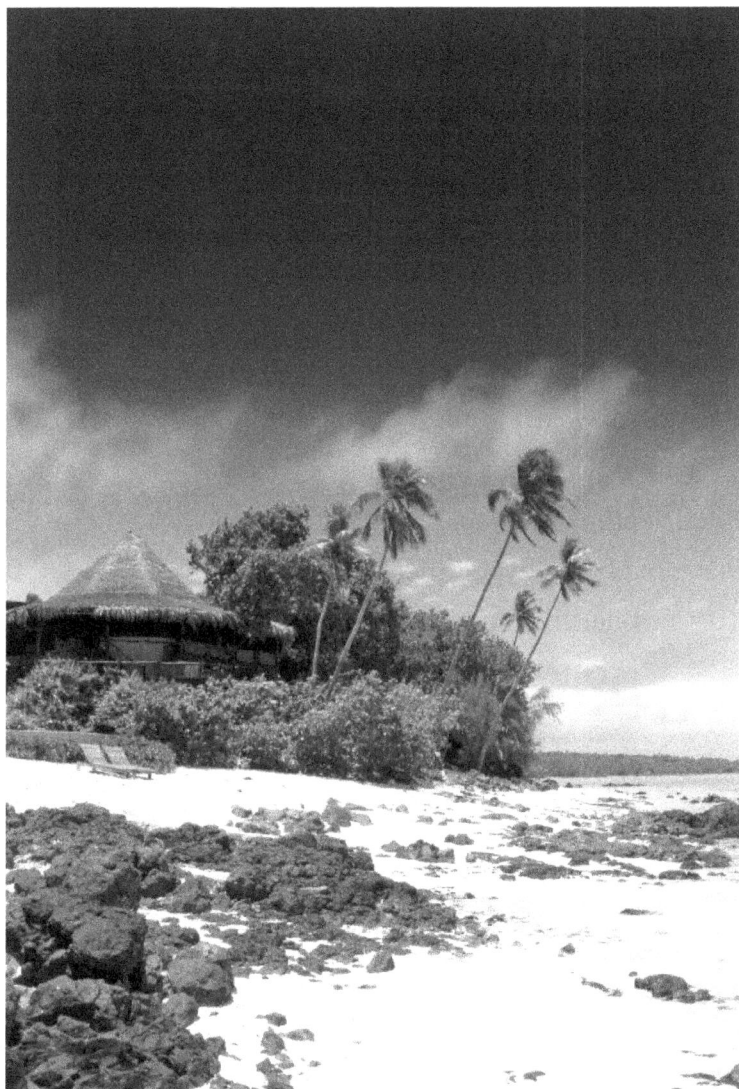

TEN POSITIVE PRECEPTS

1. Be confidential and motivating; think highly of others.

2. Eat, drink and be healthy; temperance and moderation are key factors.

3. Participate in physical exercises, either by walking or jogging; expose to fresh air.

4. Have regular worship services.

5. Endeavor to say kind words at all times.

6. Always wear a smile; be pleasant.

7. Never swear nor judge others.

8. Be compassionate, loving and forgiving.

9. Avoid being hypocritical and arrogant.

10. Consider the unfortunate ones; share your blessings.

COMPASSION

As I look around on
A people living in a world
Of disaster and hopelessness,
My heart moves with compassion.

I recall the days and years
Of human sufferings—
And even nations at large,
I yearn to help!

Leaders and followers alike
Are wondering and pondering
What will follow the great
Attack on New York City.

Thousands died in only
A day, families and friends
Are still grieving today.
Is there someone who cares?

The big question is: Will
There be peace on earth
When so many hearts are aching?
I am concerned, this is compassion.

In the midst of adversity,
It needs care and concern
To build strength and courage,
But it needs genuine compassion!

THE BUSY WOMAN

She comes to the office
Each morning even before
Anybody else does—early;
Her job seems enjoyable!

It offers much satisfaction,
She seems to like it.
It is not because labor
Is easy, it is commitment.

She hates being dependent.
She believes being independent
Is a true virtue that is
Based primarily on discipline.

Being busy is the very
Best type of medicine,
The busy woman is free from
Tensions, anxieties and stresses.

The boss she sees each day
Likes having someone he
Does not have to 'push' nor 'drive.'
She cannot be bought nor sold.

Any man who has a
Busy woman around can
Tell the world he finds
The right woman—a gift!

A HERO AT HEART!

(Owen Rhodes, Summer Camp, July 31, 1980)

*It was a shocking and frightening
Experience for all the campers,
Counselors, nurses, life-guards, and the director
Who were all at the beach that evening.*

*All the campers were taken to
The beach but we were directed
To go in the water in pairs,
What happened, I don't seem to know.*

*After several hours of struggling,
Frights, commotions, concerns and prayers,
I was rushed to the nearby hospital.
Regained consciousness, I was 'alive' again.*

*It took me a day and a night
To be treated by medical personnel
Who, in the process, told me I had drowned.
However, I was rescued by another camper.*

*Returning to camp for the
Remaining days, I discovered
That I was rescued by another
Cabin member, Owen Rhodes.*

*Although they called me 'Lazarus,'
I was overwhelmingly happy that my
Life was miraculously saved by
Divine intervention and a brave Christian hero.*

THE STRANGER

We were meeting for...
The very first time.
The stranger was busy;
I asked for the way...

The stranger was willing,
A kind individual indeed.
We smiled with each other,
Were we really strangers, though?

She looked straight in my
Humble face and said,
"We are no more strangers."
I smiled deep within.

The stranger kindly gave
The impression that she was
'An angel in disguise.'
Oh, so sure to tell....

I shivered with surprise
To know, really, that I was
Greeted and accepted by a
Stranger in a strange land.

THE BEGGAR

He comes up with a
Look of pity and
Sorrow in the face.
He waits patiently.

Then the beggar
Says, "May I have
Something to eat?
I am hungry!"

The beggar is indeed hungry.
I give without questioning;
If he should die of hunger,
I would be definitely guilty!

The beggar walks away
With great satisfaction and appreciation.
For that very moment—
The beggar's need is supplied.

I, too, am satisfied,
For when I recall—
Jesus would have done
The same for a hungry beggar.

THE 'CELL' SCENARIO.

It was a tiresome journey
From Kingston (Jamaica) on a bus,
Everybody anticipated reaching
Home early and safe.

The bus was packed to capacity.
Some of the passengers were very
Uncomfortable, suffering from cramps.
What a way to travel on a bus!

Almost every passenger had a cell phone,
The driver was no exception.
On reaching Hatfield in cool Manchester,
The driver made a sudden halt!

A few minutes later, he drove off;
He stopped the bus again.
All the passengers were in suspense.
Someone said the driver lost his 'cell.'

The driver spun the bus around
And revisited the scene of the incident.
Some bystanders were interrogated and searched
But the cellular phone was not retrieved.

SHOES

Shoes, shoes, fancy shoes,
Lovely shoes and dainty shoes,
Shoes for ladies, gentlemen and children,
Shoes in stores, shops and markets.

Cheap shoes, dear shoes,
The cobblers and the shoemakers
Made them all, for you and me;
Black shoes, brown and white shoes.

Strappy shoes, full-made shoes.
Leather and plastic shoes—
Some have buckles and laces,
But we love them all.

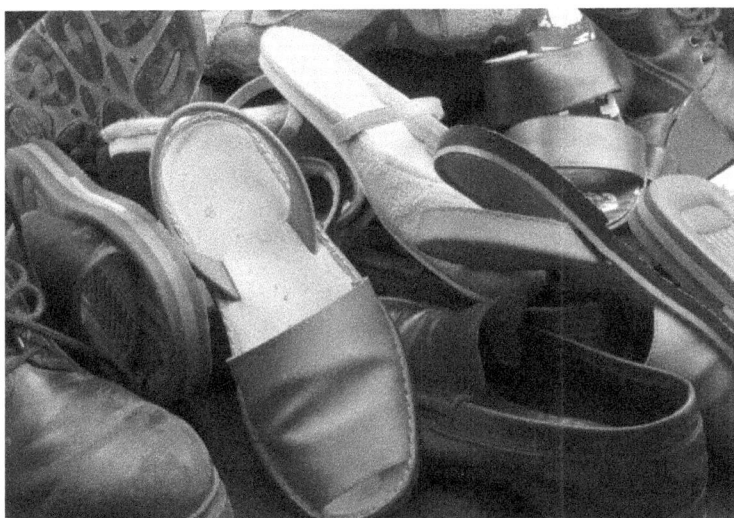

"HE IS RISEN"!

The purpose and significance
Of the Easter season is that the
Savior is risen; He is alive!
He is not in the tomb today.

The shocking discovery of the
Friends of Christ was when
They visited the place of His
Burial, but He was not there.

Through much perplexity and
Sheer disappointment, the angel
Said unto the visitors, "He is
Not here; He is risen"!

The plan of salvation is complete,
For the Savior sacrificed
Himself, over two thousand years ago,
To bring us hope of eternal life.

WHEN IT RAINED

It came to pass
In those days
That the clouds
Became extra dark!

Within a few minutes
The thunders began
To roll and lightning flashed
Sharply, all over!

Then came the rain!
It poured all evening;
Throughout the night
Into the next day.

The showers were unordinary.
The people became curious
About such phenomenon
Which was about to happen.

It was not very long
That water gushed through hills
And valleys; many homes
And other buildings flooded out!

The strangest thing happened
The people of Porus (Jamaica),
In the cool mountainous Manchester,
Have a river running through!

23

THE BUSY STREET

The street is busy
With people and traffic
Moving up and down,
Space is very limited.

Different types of vendors
Are on both sides of the street
Crying out, "Come and buy!"
Music and dances are popular.

The next person is as close
As your next step—
It is so hard to
Catch up your breath.

It is 'bumper to bumper'
Experience with both
Humans and traffic—
Combined to make a crowd.

THE TREE

The tree I see is
A naseberry tree in
The common grove;
I peer at its silvery
Color in the morning.
Yes, there is beauty in a tree.

There in the gentle wind
It seems to speak to me.
My heart is free to know
That "God is love."
For He shows Himself
In the things He made.

SIN

Sin is a serious offence.
It destroys man's eternal future.
It brings sickness and death.
It is really devastating!

Sin brings griefs and sorrows,
Sin brings aches and pains,
It causes separations and divisions,
It hurts the human psyche.

Sin is the initiator of the barrier
Between divinity and humanity.
It seeks to create numbness.
Its objectives are strange.

Sin prohibits happiness and peace.
The world lost its original
Beauty because of this venom.
The negatives were not intended.

Sin will soon be eliminated
By the Originator of righteousness;
In the hereafter, the transgression
Of God's laws will be obliterated!

AUGUST IN NATURE

The days are filled with
Fluttering butterflies moving
In unimaginable directions.
The scent of ripe mangoes
Are everywhere—so much to eat.

As day changes into night,
The bright starry sky
And the chirping of crickets
Bring home peace and rest.

Then comes a new day;
Nature is brightened with
The rising of the sun;
It is an illumination of
The blessings of summer.

FIRE

Fire is a melting element
It burns, it destroys, it kills
It has negative effects
It has positive effects

Fire is used to do good things
Fire is used to do bad things
It is used all over
The world by all people

Fire brings pains and sorrows
It is devastating and destructive
It makes life happy and comfortable
It makes life sad and uncomfortable

Fire has a divine origin
It is used for cleansing
It brings about purification
It will bring an utter end!

CHRISTMAS TIME

Christmas is a very special time
It is a time of retrospection
Yes, a time of looking back in the past
It is a season of mixed reflection

Christmas is a "countdown" time
It is the time of year when
Everybody wonders about their "yesterdays."
A time to make plans and resolutions

This special season reminds us of
The importance of giving and receiving
It is a time of reconciliation,
A time to forgive and forget

To many people Christmas
Is a holy and a joyful time
It is the season to celebrate
It is the merriest season of the year

If only the real significance
Could be maintained—'CHRIST'
Whose name builds this special time
There would be joy and peace forever!

THE ROAD TO TENNESSEE

The road to Tennessee is
Long, winding, and scary,
You travel both day and night
It seems like an endless road.

The travelers need a
Map, a chart and a
Very accurate thinking,
It is time-consuming

A halt here, a halt there
Everyone deserves a rest
After a snack or two—the
Tiresome journey continues

Traveling through the tranquil,
Quiet countryside, viewing
Breathtaking and majestic mountains
And the refreshing, green valleys

It is like playing hopscotch
Journeying from state to state—
Delaware, Maryland, and Virginia
Then to the thriving Tennessee

VICTIM OF FIRE.

The news was sudden;
It was shocking!
It was really sad,
It was like a dream!

But it was a reality,
In a few minutes the
Reality was made plain.
I saw it happened.

On the scene—
Was a large crowd
Help was hopeless
The fire was raging!

Divine Providence took
Full control so lives
Have been saved
From the wild, raging fire!

All material possessions
Went up in merciless flames,
But despite the total loss
Life still goes on.

My adrenaline had overreacted,
My heart was deeply touched.
My emotions were awakened in
Immeasurable consciousness.

I am rejoicing today,
And my testimony is open
For it is truly clear
That I am thankful for life!

THE REGGAE BOYZ

The Reggae Boyz are
Self-controlled, self-disciplined
Self-motivated and truly skillful
They are intrinsically equipped.

It is a perfect combination
Of perfect character traits
To enhance the game of
Football in a broad setting.

The Reggae Boyz have
Historically taken on an
International flavor and favor
Which is a rich heritage.

History for the Reggae Boyz
Is created out of
Sheer dedication and patriotism
This is a genuine masterpiece.

God, I am sure, will
Take this unique team
Safely on the road to France,
A great fame indeed!

The Reggae Boyz are sincere
Pace-setters whom of course
Distinctly put Jamaica
On top of the world!

REMEMBERING HURRICANE GILBERT

The warning was unheeded,
Little attention was given
To the bulletin which came
On radio and on television.

It appeared not to be
As serious as the announcers
Said it would have been;
Many people made preparations.

Clouds changed into darkness
Lightning flashed, thunder rolled
The hurricane was coming!
It was very imminent.

Then came the dreadful moment:
"The sick", "the lame" and "the lazy"
Moved with eagle's swiftness,
Everything was put to safety.

While the rains poured and
The fierce winds blew
Looters were busy out there,
They looted stores, shops, and supermarkets.

Some prayed and read
Especially Psalms 91
Their faith was strengthened
The experience was fearful.

It could be that some...
People scoffed at the power
And harsh reality of God
In disguise, Gilbert was a blessing.

Some two decades have fully dawned
It is yet another birthday
For devastating and appalling Gilbert
This has an eternal memory.

POVERTY

With shameface the poor in this
World go from door to door begging
It is no misdeed being done

It is nothing but the lack of the
Basic things of life
Scarcity of food, money and even
A proper shelter is poverty.

It is humiliating, frustrating
It is unacceptable, heart-rending
It is to be found everywhere
It knows no bounds

To the Christian and faithful
It is a blessing in disguise
To the heathen and faithless
It is an obvious curse

Poverty causes anguish and pain
Poverty causes envy and bitterness
But it was Jesus who said,
"I have the poor with Me always."

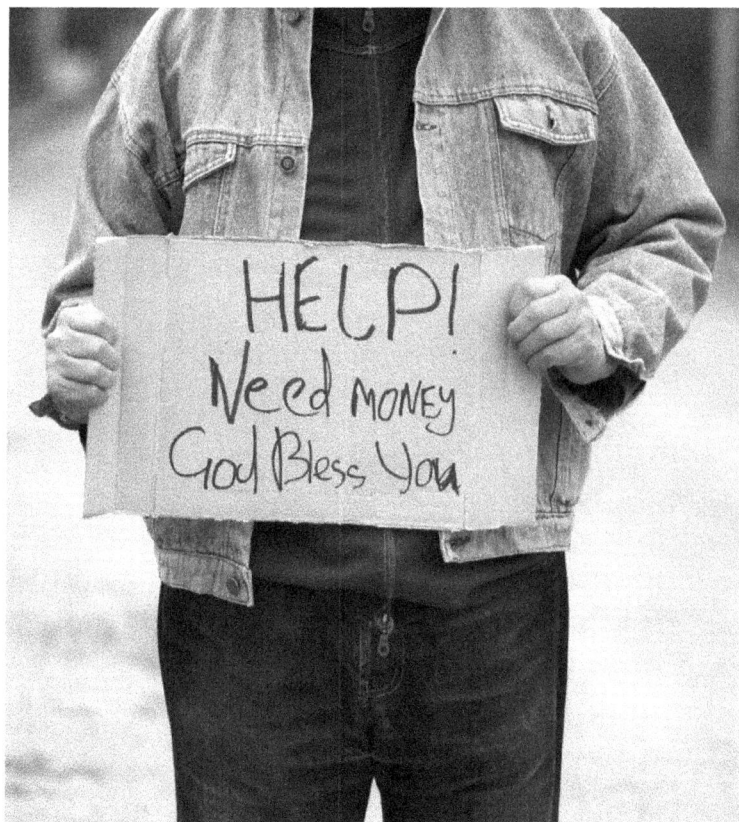

A NEW ERA

It is truly a blessing
To be awakened to face
The dawn of a new
Era—a new beginning.

The beginning of a new
Era—a new century
Is here for us to
Face its sorrowful challenges.

The new millennium
What a long-awaited time!
So it brings fears and
Doubts to many hearts?

It is just another year
With its doubled cross-roads,
Its millions and more
Miles and rugged mountains.

To the optimistic minds
There is nothing to fear
And be troubled about,
It is only nearer to eternity.

Things will change as
They do each new year
But these are inevitable
And must come to pass.

Thank goodness He
Who holds the future
Changes not, He is the
Same every new era!

Looking for peace of
Mind and sheer happiness
We will not find these
For there must be changes.

The negative things of life
Swim like oil on water,
But hardly the positive prevails
Hope is beyond tomorrow.

The new era is certainly
Here to remind us all
That it won't be too long
Before we will be going **home**.

PATIENCE

Patience is humility
Patience is longsuffering

Patience is perseverance
Patience is thinking

Patience is tolerance
Patience is time

Patience is life
Patience is powerful

Patience is endurance
*Patience keeps **one** waiting.*

LIFE'S SACRIFICES

Getting to work on time
Getting to worship on time
Being consistent with duties
It is putting priorities right.

Living up to commitments
Being here and there—
This is not quite easy
They are all life's sacrifices.

Endeavoring not to miss a date
So careful checking the diary
Fulfilling every appointment
All these are life's sacrifices.

Expressing love and compassion
To those who are in need
And giving without complaining
These are all life's sacrifices.

It is not possible to retrieve
All that is being given-
So give not to receive;
It is all life's sacrifices.

MOTHER

Mother—this name means
So much to everybody
Thinking of Mother
You think of love and care.

Mother is both the
Princess and the Queen
In the home and everywhere
She is full of love.

Mother wakes up early
In the mornings and
Works right through the day
Her labor is endless.

My mother, your mother
Is the dearest person,
Her name is everywhere
Her fame is well known.

A mother's care
Is sweeter than music
She is tender yet active
Her face expresses kindness.

The poet speaks of Mother
The author writes about her
The musician sings about her
The babe cries for her...

Mother, Mother dear,
Your love is so rare
You are so precious
You are incomparable!

LOVE

Love is a gift
From heaven, it
Needs proper nurturing
And very good care.

Love is tender and
Precious; it is great!
Love is powerful and
It should be practiced.

The love that I cherish
Has an indefinite meaning
Its significance is measureless
It knows no bounds.

Love is peaceful and calm
Love is an absolute thing
It is kind and free
Love is genuine and true.

My love, your love
Is the warmest gift
That can be shared
Between two mortal beings.

BIRDS IN POETRY

Did you know that birds generally make poetry?
Birds like the Robin, the Sparrow and the Owl
These are of varying species
The most beautiful nature speaks of

Beautiful are they when aptly described
Arranged in the mixed, gorgeous, colorful feathers
Any curious observer will notice these welcomed creatures
And be inspired while listening to their rendered tune in singing

Across the continents and islands birds are found
And with their unique manner of generosity
And attractiveness they are always heard of repeatedly by poets

Did you know that birds can be harmful
Yet helpful in their own distinct way?
On-the-vast creation there are tales of
Birds in poetry which wondered and puzzled
The minds of the young and the aged remarkably.

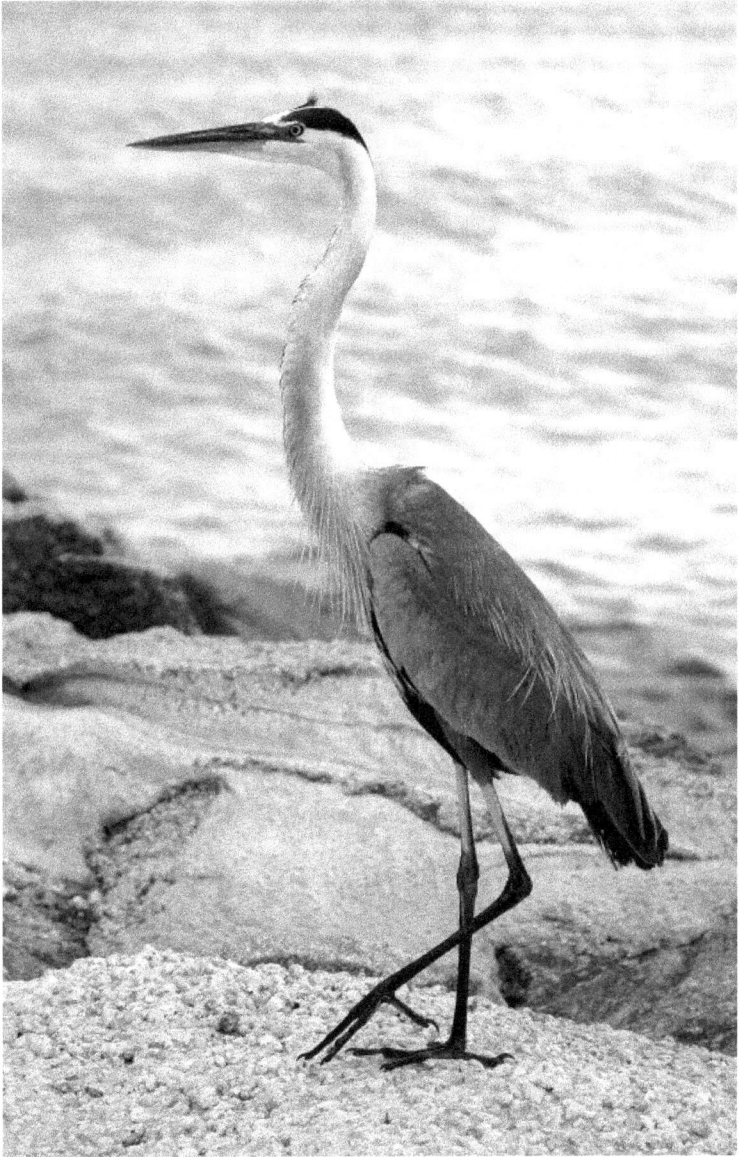

BLACKMAN

See him trudging along the
Road of poverty, toils and hardships
Your hope lies only in your Maker
Provider of all mankind

Blackman, 0 black man,
You must suffer difficulties
To survive—not because of
The color of your skin though

It is because you are a man
Of dignity, belonging and purpose
Yes, you belong to a true race,
A race of victory!

See blackman seeks
His daily bread with
Naked back, with sweat
Running down, under the hot sun.

Blackman must survive
Blackman must triumph
O Blackman, your dignity
Made you an honored specimen.

So Blackman, press on...
Your victories will soon be won
Hold your head high up
You are free, free indeed!

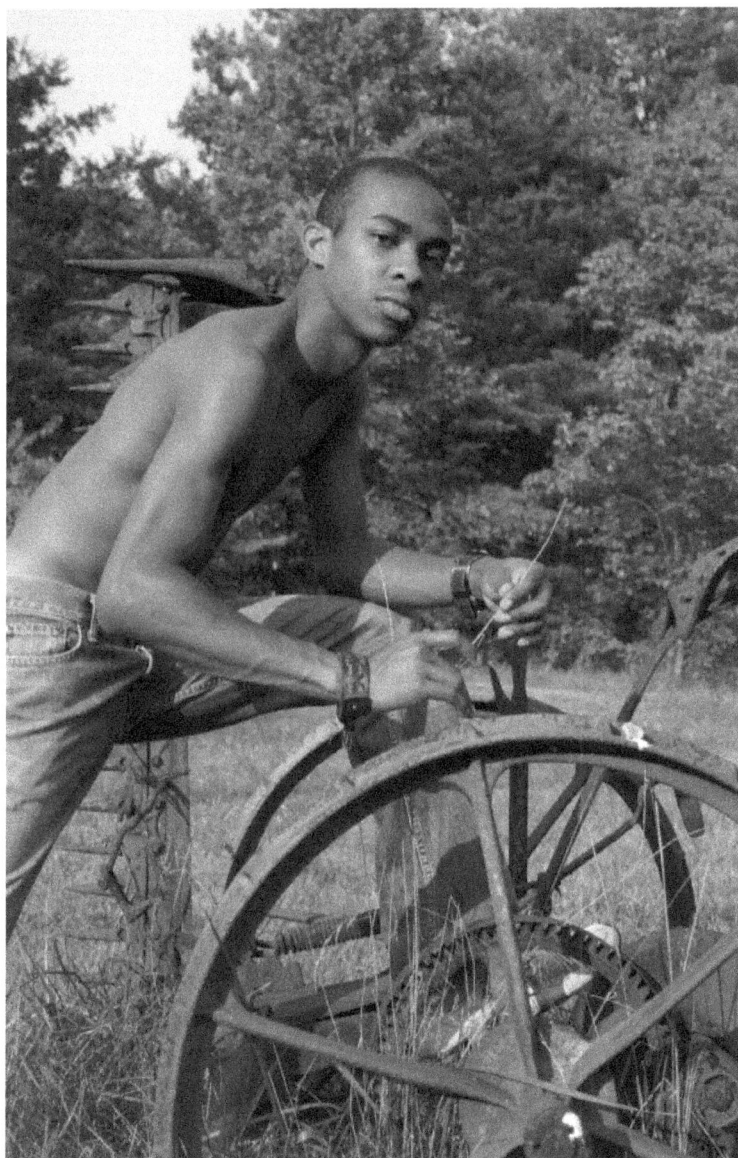

JUST BE YOURSELF

Just be yourself...
Never try to be someone else
You are you and you are unique
Being yourself is quite natural

It is real being yourself
It releases strain and stress
Because you are happy being
Just the person that you are!

Just be yourself...
Imitate no one else;
You are potentially blessed.
Just be humble... and pray

Just be yourself at...
All times, whatever it costs
Remember, you were made
Special by the 'Great I Am.'

A FRIEND

A friend is someone
Who is important indeed!
A friend is someone
Who loves and cares.

A friend always comes
In times of need to
Comfort and solace
Those they have around.

My friend and your friend
May not be the same
But they might share
Some things in common.

A friend can be of any
Age—young and old
They can be near or far
Yet they are reliable!

A friend should love at
All-times-but-some
Times they do change [but]
The Friend infinite never changes.

A MOTHER'S LOVE

A mother's love is like a rose
Its fragrance is as sweet as honey
A Mother's love knows no limit
It is as enduring as eternity

A mother's love dispels misunderstandings
And doubts, even her acquaintances
Seek after it as they seek after
Treasured gifts and rare jewels!

A mother's love is not selfish
Neither is it easily provoked;
It teaches lessons of love, peace and understanding
A mother's love is kind and forgiving

A mother's love far exceeds
Complaints and trying circumstances
Mother never complains, murmurs nor does
She grudge her own; her love is par excellence

Flowers, perfumes and gifts wrapped
Like apples of gold in pictures of silver
Cannot be compared with the love of
A mother's love to her children—loving and unloving!

CHRISTIANITY VS. "HEATHENISM"

Christianity versus 'heathenism'
In many and varying ways—
Christianity teaches and emphasizes
Moral and ethical values, and prayers.

'Heathenism' opposes moral graces
And teaches vices, evils and
Lessons of darkness and destruction;
Christianity upholds moderation and temperance.

Christianity allows freedom of worship
And give praises and honor to God;
'Heathenism' minimizes the power of God
And influences evil indulgences and passions.

Christianity emphasizes light and truth
It is the foundation of fine characters
'Heathenism' enforces laws of errors,
Indiscipline and disorderly conducts.

Christianity capitalizes on love
And forgiveness, lessons of kindness
And grace are being taught;
'Heathenism' opposes all of these.

Christianity is Christ-like behavior,
'Heathenism' is mundane and limited
Christianity offers hope of eternity,
'Heathenism' causes eternal punishment!

There is time now to choose
The better side so to be saved
From the perils of 'heathenism,'
By accepting the doctrines of Christianity.

INJUSTICE

Injustice is a painful
Experience—very painful
It brings about questionings
It causes physical, mental
Social and emotional sufferings

Injustice leaves the mind
Empty, depraved and distressed
Injustice bothers both the
Young and the aged at some
Time in their lives

Many things contribute
To injustice—robbery
Of one's privileges
Goals, achievements, families
Friends and peace of mind

The only remedy for
Injustice is fair deals
Honesty, openness, love
Understanding and genuine
Compassion—real compassion

The evil that comes
About by the spirit
Of stifling injustice
Will soon be obliterated
By the God of justice!

HIGH & LIFTED UP

I see the Savior high
And lifted up in all
His majesty and power
As He claims His own.

The Savior, the Scriptures Say,
Wins awesome victories
After which He will extend
Life eternal to His people.

"And I, if I be lifted up...,
Will draw all men unto Me,"
The Savior utters in profound
And resounding tones.

Today, in human interpretation
And simple humility, the
Sounds echo far and near
That He is being lifted up.

Our strengths are being
Renewed everyday because
The high and lifted up
Savior is our only Source.

INDISCIPLINE

Indiscipline is the inability to
Conduct oneself to climb
The ladder of success and achievement
It deters the minds of great persons.

Indiscipline causes injury
To a person's moral, ethical
Educational and spiritual developments
It cripples an individual or a nation

Any person who demonstrates
Indisciplined attitudes brings
Discouragements to his families,
Authorities and familiar friends.

The indisciplined person or persons
Lose focus of his goals and
Personal achievements; his
Focus is on negative thoughts.

He who believes in falsehood
Will reap the harvest of bitterness;
Indiscipline bears no good fruits,
It brings despair and failures

It might take the disciplinarian
A million years to accomplish
The task of opposing indiscipline
But the results might be infinite.

EXPLOITATION OF THE POOR

We are indeed living
In the very last days,
We do not seem to care
About others any more.

The less fortunate ones
Are constantly being exploited
By the wealthier ones.
How unfortunate it is!

Some people use diplomacy
And psychology to oppress
Those who can barely survive,
This is a sign of the time.

In every sphere of society,
Dishonesty and lack of
Integrity exist—it ...
Is a question—Who cares?

THE FUNERAL

The funeral—it is a
Time of grief, a time
To weep and mourn
It is a time of sorrows.

At the funeral, tears
Sometimes flow and
Relatives and friends
Share mixed emotions.

One wonders how so
Many things happen at
The funeral, being a very
Sad occasion for the mourners

Old time friends get
The chance to meet and
Greet each other again
It is a time to reconcile!

The funeral—it is a
Time to express sympathies,
Sing, comfort and extend
Love and kindness to
The bereaved ones.

Cameramen with cameras
Of different sorts and brands,
Videos and the like, are busy
Taking pictures, no one escapes!

The most serious part
However, of the funeral, is
The sermon or the spoken word,
Attention is in full focus!

It is a time to
Reflect on past mistakes
And time appropriate
To strive to be right!

Some people pray very
Special prayers, while
Some become stronger in
The things of God and heaven.

THE SNOB!

The snob always
Tries to humiliate
Those who are not
It is believed the same

The snob thinks and says
All but good about
Anyone who falls prey
In unfortunate situations

The snob never tries
To be honest with others
The snob, instead,
Rules with underestimation

All is 'handicapped'
For the snob and
No one else is capable
Of doing things right

Whatever the snob does
Or whatever the snob thinks
It has no meaning
Except just being snobbish!

THE ARMY MAN

In a world of 'modern'
Technology and easy living
A few young people are
Living it the tough way!

Life in the Army is not
Easy, but a few loyal
Young people are in it.
They are the chosen few.

The man in the Army
Is a very active one—
He is a chef, a businessman, a driver
An explorer and an architect, too.

The man in the Army
Is young but responsible;
He is a family oriented
Character of great experiences.

The man in the Army
Is an influential person
He is a genuine role model
And a sincere leader!

VICTIM OF DISAPPOINTMENTS

Life filled with disappointments
Can be very heart-rending
There are disappointments with
Relatives, friends and associates

There are disappointments
With plans, health and goals
Life from its beginning has been
Covered with clouds of disappointments

Some disappointments are
Passed and gone and some are here to stay
There are disappointments in and out
These make each moment sadder

There are disappointments in the home,
School, and in college
There are disappointments in the working world—why?
Yes, I am a victim of disappointments.

RIPE BANANAS
CONTRASTED PINEAPPLES

Bananas and pineapples
Are edible fruits;
They are nutritious
Fruits of much delight.

The ripe bananas have
A golden, bright color
Whose exterior texture
Is smooth and freckled.

In contrast to the pineapple,
The ripe bananas
Can be eaten readily
As well as making a refreshing drink.

These fruits are healthy
For the body's growth
And can be eaten
Any time of the day.

FRIENDS

Friends are true
Friends are false
Friends are faithful
Friends are failure

Friends are reliable
Friends are trustworthy
Friends are persecuting
Friends are confidential

Friends are near
Friends are far
The friendship that is bound
By true love will last forever.

UNTIMELY DEATH?

He was enjoying life
For the very last time.
The blow was sudden;
It was severe and fatal.

What was lying there?
It was someone dying.
He was critically injured.
Could his life be spared?

This was the child of
Another family who was
Unprepared to face...
The reality of death.

Did he know he would die
So young and so sudden?
It was an accident—
But why did he have to die?

Everybody was in suspense
Of him being really dead.
It was hard to believe
That death is so cruel.

The news hit the air
Not very long after,
The youth is dead.
They all wept bitterly!

LIFE IS...

Life is filled with inspirations
It tells of fortunes and aspirations
It is filled with significance...
And lots of achievements!

Life is living today—
And having high
Expectations for the future,
And its dreams and realities

Life is real, live it!
Life is good, accept it!
Life is making the
Best use of everything.

Life is not "a bed of roses,"
Life is like a tale that
Is told of all its
Positive and negative realities.

Life is filled with experiences.
Life is like a vapor...
It is present today and
Tomorrow it is gone, gone...!

CHILDREN

Who are called children?
Children are God's heritage;
They are special gifts –
Made by God Himself.

How do children come about?
It is an intimate relationship
Between a male and a female
And the fusion of the ovum and spermatozoón

Children are born in the world
As innocent beings who need
Proper care and individual attention;
They need parental guidance.

Children need love and affection
Just as much as food;
They have great potentials,
And are able to make choices.

Think about the world without children –
It would be a dull place,
Children bring life and light to this
World and make it a better place.

GRACE

Grace is distinctly the favor
God bestows on humanity;
A gift that we do not deserve
Grace is God's divine mercy.

Grace is an infinite virtue
Extended to a fallen generation.
It is the power to overcome
Trials, temptations and difficulties.

Grace is the kindness given
To a fallen race a long time ago.
Faithful Noah found grace in
The eyes of the Lord.

We, like the apostle Paul,
Should claim a fresh supply
Of the grace of God which
Is sufficient to keep us daily.

REFLECTION

Remembering...

K *ind and courteous.*

H *ad great potentials*

Y *earned for an eternal trophy.*

O *ne and only.*

N *eat at all times.*

E *ndeavored to excel.*

S *tudious.*

T *ender-hearted.*

E *ducated to serve.*

W *illing to lead.*

A *rticulate and ambitious.*

R *eligious.*

T *houghtful and trustworthy.*

Author's note: As a result of a motor vehicle accident, Khyone Stewart passed away on May 24, 2009. (He is 'gone too soon').

THE HEREAFTER

I have no need to fear,
For the days are long ever.
Within are inexperienced joys,
I need not suffer hunger nor pain.

There are no nights, only days.
My daily repast is sure,
I need not plan for tomorrow,
For today will be forever.

Gone are bitterness and resentment,
Hypocrisy and grudge are ceased,
No crying at any funeral service,
The causes of sin are now obliterated.

My families and friends are happy,
And all are enjoying a new life.
The animals and birds all play along,
Within is oneness and sheer togetherness.

The streets are paved with gold,
And the citizens walk freely about.
There are no bills to pay,
For it is a new life indeed.

I am glad for this new experience,
For all my debts are paid,
Every child and adult here
Enjoys inexpressible freedom.

www.ingramcontent.com/pod-product-compliance
Lightning Source LLC
Chambersburg PA
CBHW060440090426
42733CB00011B/2349